XTREME UNIVERSE

BLACK HOLES

AND MORE DARK MYSTERIES

A&D Xtreme
BOLD HI-LO NONFICTION
An imprint of Abdo Publishing
abdobooks.com

ANN WILLIAMS

TAKE IT TO THE XTREME!

GET READY FOR AN EXTREME ADVENTURE! THE PAGES OF THIS BOOK WILL TAKE YOU INTO THE THRILLING WORLD OF ASTRONOMICAL WONDERS. WHEN YOU HAVE FINISHED READING THIS BOOK, TAKE THE XTREME CHALLENGE ON PAGE 45 ABOUT WHAT YOU'VE LEARNED!

ABDOBOOKS.COM
Published by Abdo Publishing, a division of ABDO, PO Box 398166, Minneapolis, Minnesota 55439.

Printed in the United States of America, North Mankato, MN.
102024
012025

THIS BOOK CONTAINS RECYCLED MATERIALS

Design: Kelly Doudna, Mighty Media, Inc.
Production: Mighty Media, Inc.
Editor: Katherine Chu

Cover Photograph: NASA/JPL-Caltech
Interior Photographs: AIP Emilio Segrè Visual Archives, courtesy of Martin Schwarzschild/Wikimedia Commons, p. 16; Baperookamo/Wikimedia Commons, pp. 34–35; Damian Lugowski/Shutterstock Images, pp. 6–7; DOE/FNAL/DECam/R. Hahn/CTIO/NOIRLab/NSF/AURA, pp. 42–43; EHT Collaboration, pp. 30–31, 32; ESA, Hubble/Wikimedia Commons, pp. 18–19; ESO/L. Calçada, pp. 20–21; Ferdinand Schmutzer/Wikimedia Commons, p. 17; Godfrey Kneller/Wikimedia Commons, p. 7; NASA and H. Richer (University of British Columbia), pp. 36–37; NASA/CXC/Ecole Polytechnique Federale de Lausanne, Switzerland/D.Harvey & NASA/CXC/Durham Univ/R.Massey (X-ray); NASA, ESA, D. Harvey (Ecole Polytechnique Federale de Lausanne, Switzerland) and R. Massey (Durham University, UK) (Optical & Lensing Map), pp. 40–41; NASA/CXC/SAO/Ákos Bogdan (X-ray); NASA/ESA/CSA/STScI (Infrared), pp. 26–27; NASA, ESA, CSA, STScI, J. Diego (Instituto de Física de Cantabria, Spain), J. D'Silva (U. Western Australia), A. Koekemoer (STScI), J. Summers & R. Windhorst (ASU), and H. Yan (U. Missouri), pp. 38–39; NASA, ESA, SSC, CXC, STScI, pp. 32–33; NASA's Goddard Space Flight Center/Jeremy Schnittman, pp. 28–29; NASA/JPL-Caltech, pp. 1, 10–11, 14–15, 44; NASA/JPL-Caltech/DSS, pp. 22–23; NASA/JPL/USGS, pp. 8–9; NRAO/AUI/NSF/NASA, pp. 12–13; Sloan Digital Sky Survey, pp. 24–25; Vadim Sadovski/Shutterstock Images, pp. 4–5
Design Elements: Arafat/Adobe Stock (header background); pixel/Adobe Stock (universe); Sergey Nivens/Shutterstock Images (header background)

LIBRARY OF CONGRESS CONTROL NUMBER: 2024938311
PUBLISHER'S CATALOGING-IN-PUBLICATION DATA
Names: Williams, Ann, author.
Title: Black holes and more dark mysteries / by Ann Williams
Description: Minneapolis, Minnesota : ABDO Publishing, 2025 | Series: Xtreme universe | Includes online resources and index.
Identifiers: ISBN 9781098295035 (lib. bdg.) | ISBN 9798384915089 (ebook)
Subjects: LCSH: Black holes (Astronomy)--Juvenile literature. | Frozen stars--Juvenile literature. | Universe--Juvenile literature. | Outer space--Exploration--Juvenile literature. | Astronomy--Juvenile literature.
Classification: DDC 523.112--dc23

CONTENTS

CHAPTER 1

REAL OR FICTION?

You are peacefully exploring outer space in your spacecraft. Suddenly, you feel the ship being dragged toward a huge, dark circle in space. You try to **steer** away from it, but it's no use. You are being sucked into a black hole!

Getting pulled into a black hole is a common feature of science fiction stories. This has never happened to a real spacecraft. But black holes do exist. They are the darkest things in the universe!

Characters in science fiction stories sometimes use black holes to travel through time or as portals to other universes.

CHAPTER 2

WHAT IS A BLACK HOLE?

A black hole is an area of space that has **extremely** strong gravity. Gravity is a natural force that pulls other things toward the center of an object. Earth's gravity is what causes things to fall to the ground. And it keeps people and objects from floating up into the sky.

Sir Isaac Newton discovered gravity in the mid-1660s. Many believe he developed the theory of gravity after watching an apple fall from a tree.

The moon's gravity is six times weaker than Earth's gravity.

Every object has gravity. But the strength of the force varies. For example, the moon's gravity is weaker than Earth's. So, astronauts are able to jump much higher on the moon than on Earth.

XTREME FACT

Astronaut Neil Armstrong's space suit weighed 81 pounds (36.7 kg) on Earth. On the moon, it weighed 30 pounds (13.6 kg).

A black hole has the strongest gravity in the universe. It pulls in anything that comes too close. A black hole's gravity is so strong that it can pull in objects that are millions of miles away!

A black hole's gravity is so strong, it can pull in stars and planets.

XTREME FACT

When a black hole pulls on an object, it tears the object apart into spaghetti-like strands. Scientists call this *spaghettification*.

CHAPTER 3

OBSERVING BLACK HOLES

Black holes are dark because the gravity is so strong that light gets pulled in and can't escape. This means that we can't actually see black holes. We see things when light bounces off them and into our eyes. Since light can't bounce off black holes, they are **invisible** to the human eye!

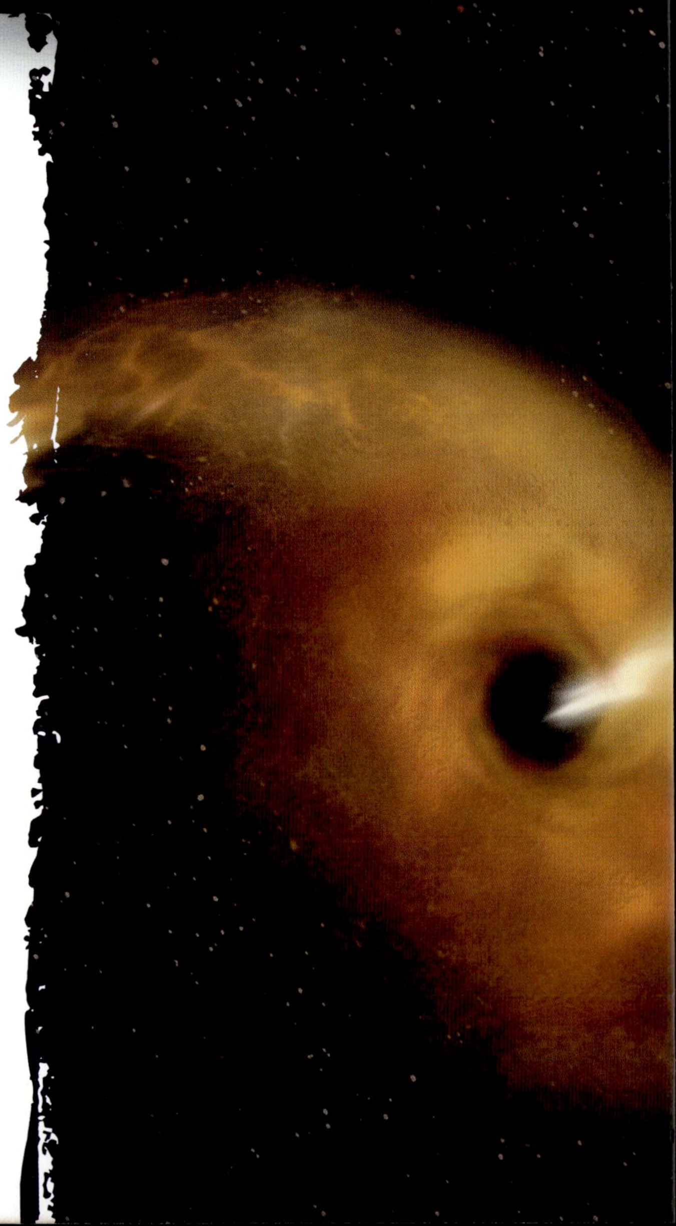

When a black hole tears a star apart, it creates a long stream of hot gas. This is known as a tidal disruption event.

Gas gets hotter as it's pulled by a black hole. The hottest spot near a black hole is called the corona. It's located above the center and made of a cloud of plasma.

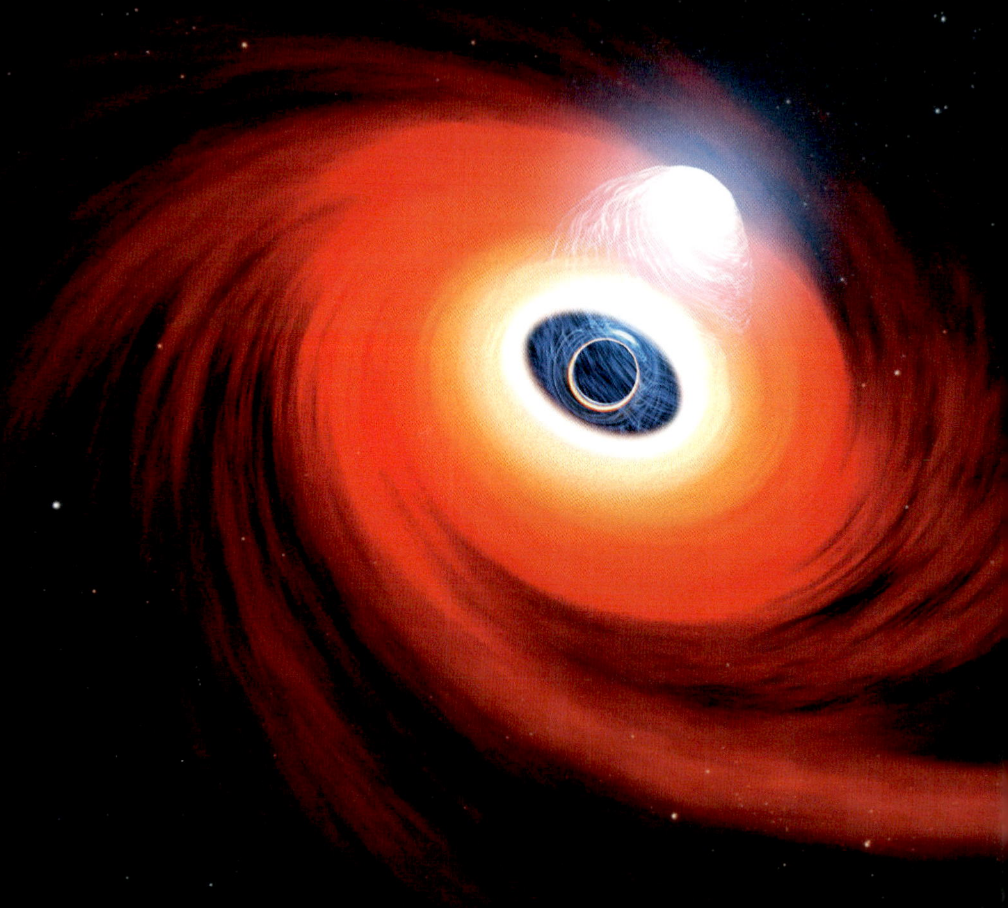

Scientists use special telescopes to observe black holes. They find where black holes are located by watching the behavior of stars. A star being pulled by a black hole gets very hot, so it glows extra bright. This can indicate that a black hole is near the star.

CHAPTER 4

BLACK HOLE HISTORY

German astronomer Karl Schwarzschild further developed the work of Michell.

In the 1700s, British scientist John Michell came up with the idea that black holes existed. Michell was studying light and gravity. He realized that it might be possible for a star to have enough gravity that light couldn't escape from it.

In 1915, Albert Einstein showed that the gravity of large objects in space bends space and time. Smaller objects are pulled toward larger objects because the large objects pull space-time toward themselves.

Cygnus X-1 (*right*) pulls in materials from a big blue star next to it. With the help of multiple telescopes, scientists are still studying Cygnus X-1 today.

Cygnus X-1 was the first black hole to be identified. It was first detected in 1964. But Cygnus X-1 wasn't confirmed to be a black hole until the 1990s.

XTREME FACT

The term *black hole* was first used in the 1960s by American scientist John Wheeler.

CHAPTER 5

HOW BLACK HOLES FORM

There are several different types of black holes. Most black holes form from dying stars. When a star dies, its **core collapses** and it explodes in a **supernova**. If the star is big enough, the core will continue to collapse, becoming a **stellar** black hole. Stellar black holes are 3 to 50 times bigger than the sun.

The European Southern Observatory discovered a stellar black hole (*left*) in the spiral galaxy NGC 300 in 2010. It had a mass that was 20 times greater than the sun's.

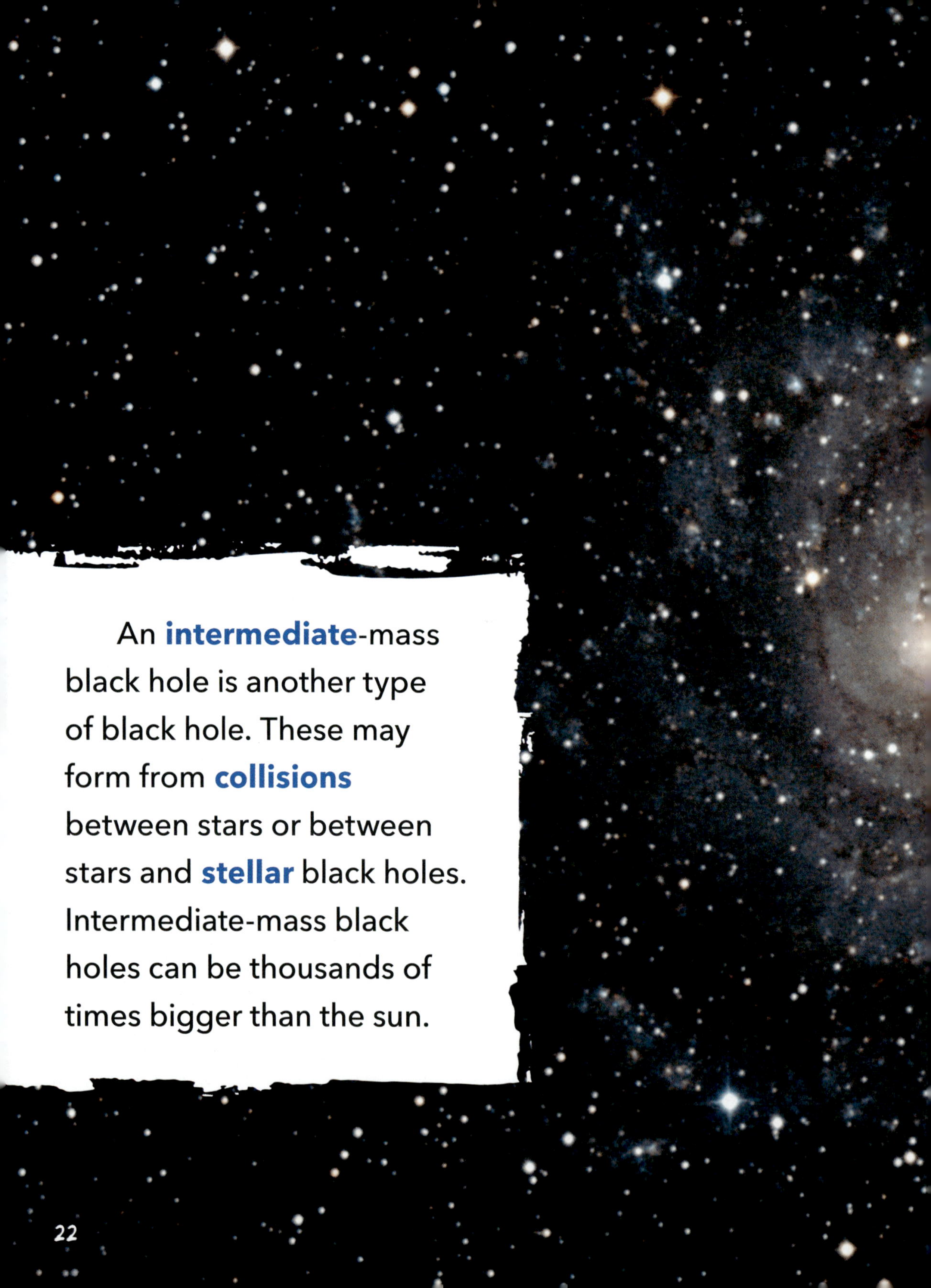

An **intermediate**-mass black hole is another type of black hole. These may form from **collisions** between stars or between stars and **stellar** black holes. Intermediate-mass black holes can be thousands of times bigger than the sun.

In 2013, NASA spotted two possible intermediate-mass black holes (*pink spots*). Scientists think they may be intermediate-mass black holes because they are brighter than stellar black holes.

The largest type of black hole is known as a **supermassive** black hole. Scientists aren't sure how they form. But they know most **galaxies** have supermassive black holes at their centers. Earth is in the Milky Way galaxy. The Milky Way has a supermassive black hole called Sagittarius A*, pronounced "Sagittarius A star."

As of 2023, Ton 618 (*blue spot*) is the largest supermassive black hole ever found. Its mass is 66 billion times greater than the sun's mass.

In 2023, scientists discovered a black hole about 13.2 billion light-years away using X-rays (*left*) and infrared data (*right*). Scientists believe the black hole formed 470 million years after the big bang.

There could be a fourth type of black hole called a **primordial** black hole. This would be the smallest variety of black holes. Scientists haven't proven that they exist. But they believe some areas in space had **extremely** hot and **dense materials** during the **big bang**. These materials could have **collapsed**, forming primordial black holes.

CHAPTER 6

EVENT HORIZON TELESCOPE

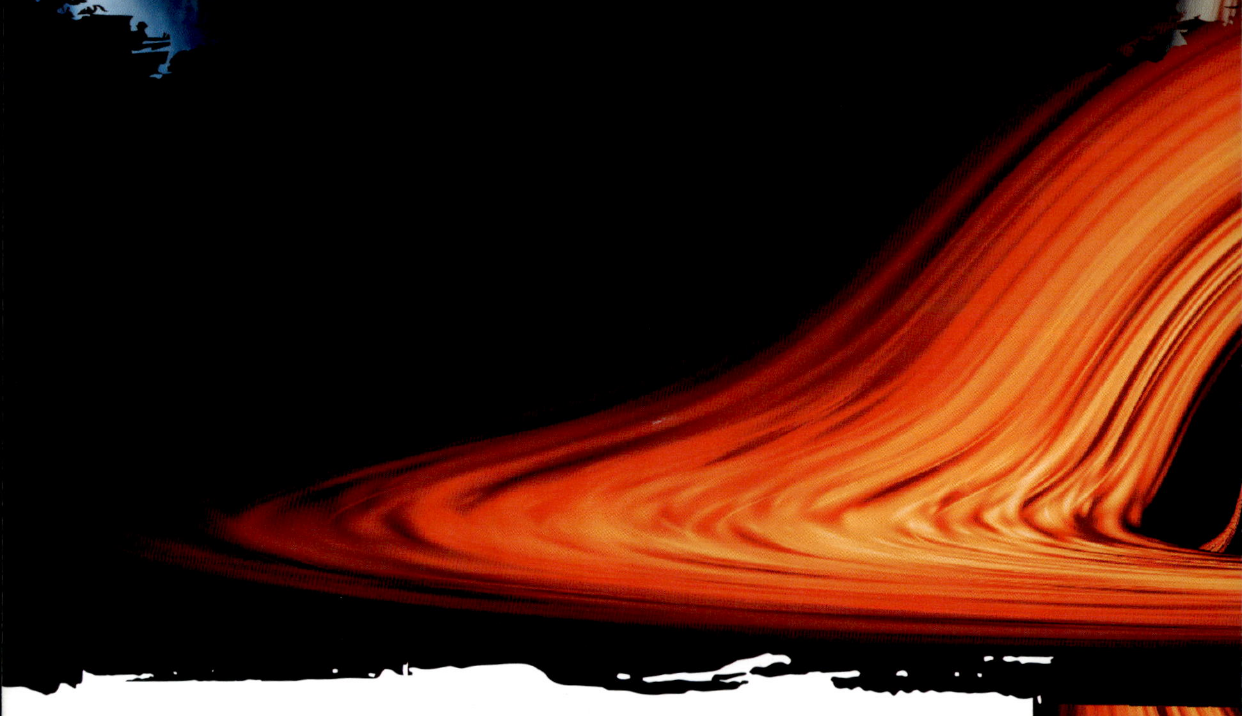

In 2009, scientists established the Event Horizon Telescope (EHT) to study black holes. Every black hole has an event horizon. This is the boundary where light is still visible before it's sucked into a black hole. Because light can be seen at the edge of the event horizon, it forms an outline of the black hole.

Once light passes through the event horizon into a black hole, it cannot escape. Because of this, scientists are unable to see past the event horizon.

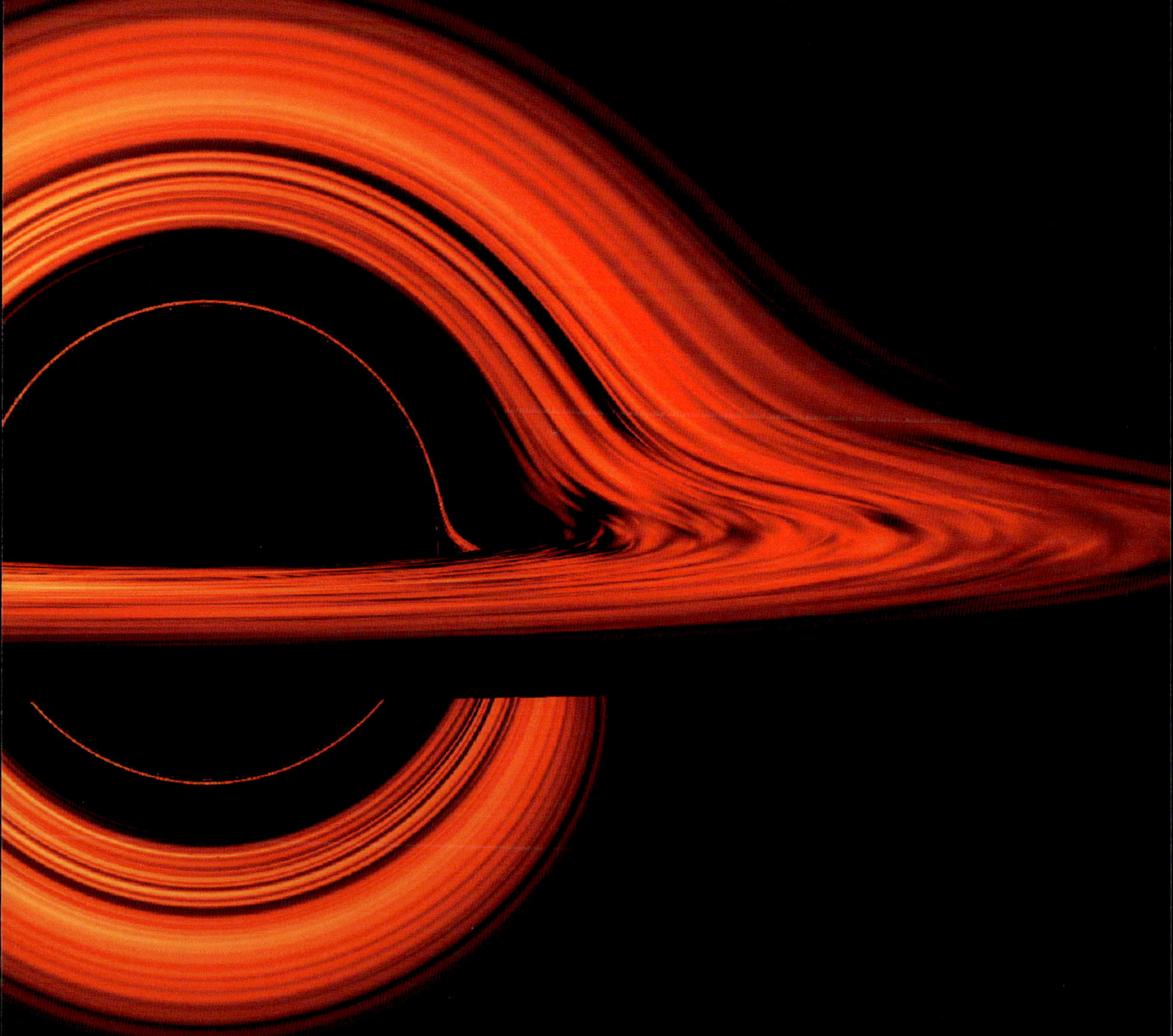

The EHT is a **network** of telescopes around the world working together. Pictures and data from the telescopes are sent to Cambridge, Massachusetts, and Bonn, Germany, to be studied. In 2019, the EHT produced the first images of a black hole in a **galaxy** called Messier 87.

In 2021, the EHT released a new image of the supermassive black hole in the Messier 87 galaxy.

In 2022, the EHT produced the first images of the Milky Way's black hole. The images confirmed that Sagittarius A* is indeed a **supermassive** black hole. Scientists hope to use data from the EHT to learn more about supermassive black holes.

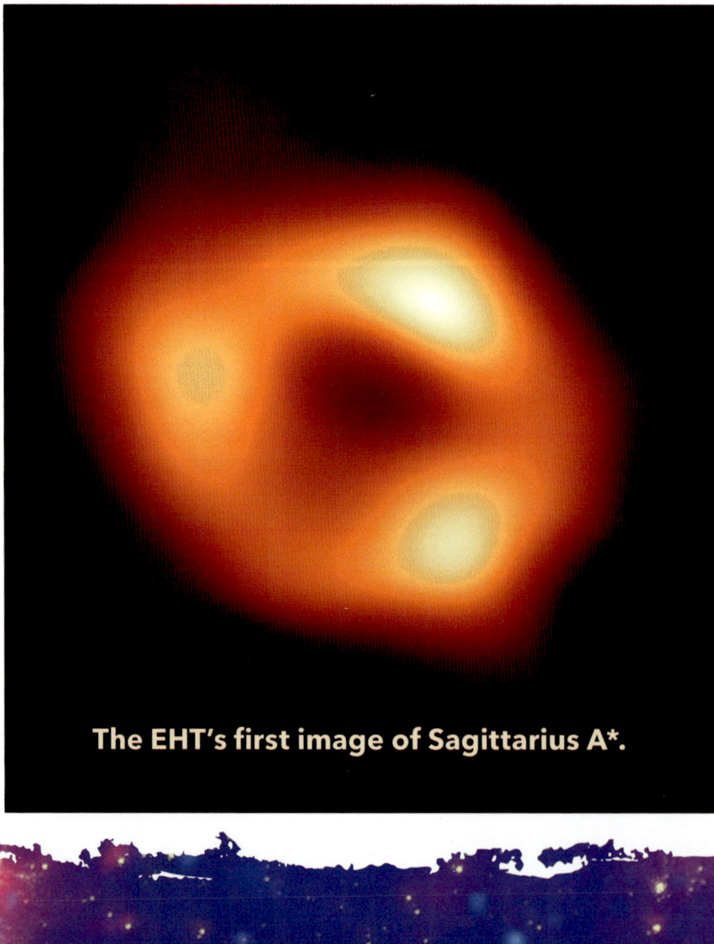

The EHT's first image of Sagittarius A*.

Sagittarius A* is surrounded by swirling hot gas (*bright white swirl*). Even though Sagittarius A* is about 27,000 light-years away, it is the closest supermassive black hole to Earth.

CHAPTER 7

BLACK DWARFS

Black holes are the darkest things in the universe. But there are many other dark objects in space. These include black dwarfs. A black dwarf is a star in its final stage. This is when a star eventually stops **emitting** heat and light and becomes cold and black.

Only the biggest stars explode into supernovas when they die. Most stars burn out over many millions of years. Scientists believe they will eventually freeze, becoming black dwarfs.

However, scientists have not found proof of a black dwarf yet. So, it's still a **theory**. Scientists think the process of becoming a black dwarf could take quadrillions of years. The universe is about 14 billion years old, so there hasn't been enough time for black dwarfs to form.

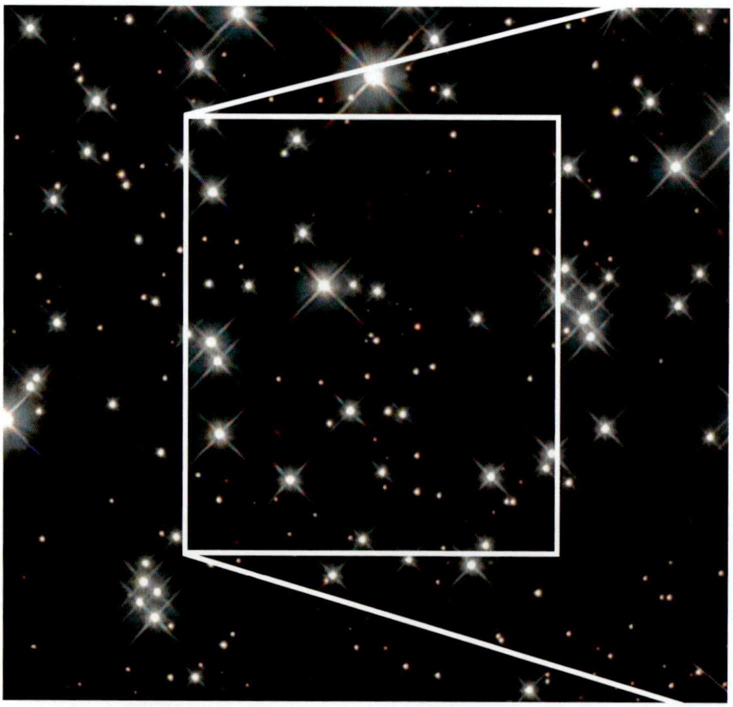

XTREME FACT

There are 1,000 millions in one billion, 1,000 billions in one trillion, and 1,000 trillions in one quadrillion.

White dwarfs (*circled*) in the Milky Way galaxy. A smaller star becomes a white dwarf when it runs out of fuel. When it burns out, it becomes a black dwarf.

CHAPTER 8

DARK MATTER AND DARK ENERGY

Galaxies, stars, planets, and other space objects make up just a small part of the universe. These objects are made of **normal** matter. Normal matter is made of atoms with protons, neutrons, and electrons. Only about 5 percent of the universe is made of normal matter.

The galaxy cluster MACS0416 is about 4.3 billion light-years from Earth. Scientists consider this photo of MACS0416 to be one of the most colorful images of the universe ever taken.

Scientists don't know exactly what the rest of the universe is made of. But they know it's different from **normal** matter. They also know that about 27 percent of the universe is matter that has gravity but doesn't **emit** any light or energy. Scientists call this dark matter.

Telescopes and sensors can't detect dark matter (*blue*). But astronomers can find it based on how it affects other objects in space. For example, dark matter could be responsible for the unexplained movement of stars.

Dark energy is a force that pushes against gravity. This force causes the universe to expand. Scientists use the Dark Energy Camera (*pictured*) to measure the growth of the universe.

Scientists also know the universe is **expanding**. They don't know what is causing this expansion but believe it is some type of energy. They call it dark energy.

The remaining 68 percent of the universe is made of dark energy. Like dark matter, dark energy is **undetectable**. But scientists believe it exists because of how it affects the growth of the universe.

CHAPTER 9

DARK MYSTERIES

The darkest things in the universe include black holes, black dwarfs, dark matter, and dark energy. They are so dark that they are hard to see and study. But scientists continue to try to learn more about these mysteries.

Black holes can't be photographed directly. NASA provides a program in which artists can illustrate what black holes may look like.

XTREME CHALLENGE

TAKE THE QUIZ BELOW AND PUT WHAT YOU'VE LEARNED TO THE TEST!

1) Who first had the idea that black holes exist?

2) Have you ever done an experiment about gravity?

3) What are the different types of black holes?

4) How much of the universe is made up of normal matter?

5) Would you want to help with the search for black holes?

GLOSSARY

big bang–the explosion that created the universe.

collapse–to suddenly break down or to cave in.

collision–a forceful crashing together of two objects.

core–the center of a space object such as a planet, moon, or star.

dense–having parts very close together.

emit–to give off or out.

expand–to get bigger. Expansion is the act of getting bigger.

extremely–to a degree that exceeds the ordinary or expected.

galaxy–a very large group of stars, planets, and other objects in space.

intermediate–in the middle or between two extremes.

invisible–not able to be seen.

material–what a thing is made up of.

network–a group of people or devices made up of many interdependent or related parts.

normal—most common.

primordial—earliest in existence.

steer—to guide or control.

stellar—related to the stars.

supermassive—having a very large amount of mass.

supernova—a star that explodes and gives off a large amount of energy.

theory—a general rule offered to explain a scientific event.

undetectable—not able to be seen or discovered.

ONLINE RESOURCES

Booklinks
NONFICTION NETWORK
FREE! ONLINE NONFICTION RESOURCES

To learn more about black holes, please visit **abdobooklinks.com** or scan this QR code. These links are routinely monitored and updated to provide the most current information available.

INDEX